# The Spectrum of Responsibility

Peter A. French

*Lennox Distinguished Professor*
*Trinity University*
*San Antonio, Texas*

**ST. MARTIN'S PRESS**
New York

*Project management:* The Book Studio, Inc.
*Cover design:* Doug Steel

Library of Congress Catalog Card Number: 89-63895
Copyright © 1991 by St. Martin's Press, Inc.
Manufactured in the United States of America.
54321
fedcba

For information, write:
St. Martin's Press, Inc.
175 Fifth Avenue
New York, NY 10010

ISBN: 0-312-03496-2

# Preface

In our everyday dealings with each other the concept of responsibility, in various guises, plays a major role. We talk of being responsible, holding people responsible, having responsibilities, avoiding responsibility, being a responsible person, and so on. To grasp the intricacies of moral discourse, an understanding of the range of the concept of responsibility is surely essential.

This book begins by examining the centrality of responsibility ascription in our social lives. How radically different would our world be were we not to have the concept of responsibility? It is crucial to our practices of punishing, compensating, and blaming. In such a world we would have to create alternative practices to deal with our communal concerns. For example, a no-fault compensation scheme for all injuries might be adopted, but to do so would bring very real costs, both economic and moral, to the way we conduct our lives. The second chapter examines historically influential analyses of responsibility. Aristotle associates responsibility with voluntary action, which for him includes acts of anger, desire, and impulse. He also holds people responsible for their characters, a view discussed in more detail in Chapter 7. J. L. Austin, using an approach much influenced by Aristotle, examines the ways we get on and off the responsibility hook. Bradley links the concept of responsibility to that of liability to punishment, and in doing so explicates three conditions for moral responsibility. Those conditions depend upon a theory of personal identity, an ownership theory of action, and a doctrine of moral personhood.

Chapter 3 continues a discussion on which Bradley focuses: the relationship between responsibility and freedom. Chapter 4 exposes and distinguishes many of the varieties of responsibility found in ordinary and professional discourse, and the principles that are used when ascribing or assigning responsibility. Chapter 5 examines the puzzling problem of whether, and when, people should be held responsible for their failures to act.

Because blaming is one of the major practices that depends on the concept of responsibility and is often identified with it, Chapter 6 investigates what it is to blame, and how blaming functions in our moral conceptual world.

The last three chapters concern the expansion of the spectrum of responsibility into the problematic areas of the criminal law, collective action, and the corporate world.

This book is intended to enhance the reader's grasp of the underlying metaphysical and ethical issues and theories that affect our thinking about responsibility. With the exception of works by Aristotle, Bradley, and Hume, the discussions focus on twentieth-century writers. One explanation is that the famous moral theorists of the Western philosophical tradition did not direct their attention to the concept. It tends to play a supporting role to their discussions of right, wrong, good, and duty. The term itself only emerges in the literature in the late eighteenth century. Contemporary philosophers have come to appreciate the complexity of the concept and to explore the scope of its uses in moral, political, social, and legal discourse.

Several people have made significant contributions to the development of this book. I remain especially indebted to my teachers, H. D. Lewis, J. L. Mackie, and Donald Davidson. Kurt Baier's influence is very real, as is that of Herbert Fingarette. I have had invaluable discussions on the topics of various chapters with Virginia Held, David Pears, John Ladd, Larry May, David Cooper, Lisa Newton, Thomas Donaldson, Thomas Dunfee, Rex Martin, and Michael Zimmerman. I owe a special thanks to Robert Curtis for his insightful comments on earlier drafts. Three groups of participants in the National Endowment for the Humanities Summer Seminar for College Teachers played major roles in shaping the selections and what I have to say about them. I wish to thank the National Endowment for supporting my directorship of those seminars in 1983, 1987, and 1990 on various subjects within the spectrum of responsibility.

I am particularly grateful to my secretary, Virginia Redford, who struggled to read my handwritten pages and produced clean and accurate copy from them.

I would like to thank the following St. Martin's Press reviewers: Patrick Derr, Clark University; David Mayo, University of Minnesota-Duluth; Norman Melchert, Lehigh University; Jennifer Moore, University of Delaware; Robert Paul, Reed College; James Roper, Michigan State University; Steven Sverdlik, Southern Methodist University; and Harry van der Linden, University of North Carolina.

Finally my wife Sandra was an invaluable sounding board and unfailing critic of style.

# Contents

# Chapter 1

# A World without Responsibility

Imagine a world without responsibility, a world in which no one is ever held legally or morally responsible for anything that happens. In that world there is no moral accounting, no blaming, no heaping on of praise, no accumulating of credit for what people do. It sounds like a great place, a no-fault world in which no one is accredited as a responsible person and in which no one has any responsibilities. But what would it be like to live in such a world? What else do we lose, when we toss out responsibility?

The world without responsibility surely tempts us because we spend much of our time in various efforts to avoid or lessen personal responsibility. If there is one thing common to us with respect to responsibility, it's that most of the time we'd rather not have it. You take it. Our language is rife with expressions used to get us off the hook, to "pass the buck," to excuse our harm-causing actions. What is it that we so often seek to dodge? What would be missing in a world that didn't have it? Could such a world support a moral system and a stable society? To answer those questions we first need to get an understanding of the basic structure of responsibility ascription.

Consider the following examples based on real or fictional situations:

1.   Hanna, a Polish Jew, was transported to a death camp in 1942. She was the mother of two children, twins, whom she dearly loved. Her husband was killed in the uprising in the Warsaw ghetto. After disembarking from the train, she and her children were brought before the camp commander. He told her that she would work as a servant in his house, but that only one of the twins could live and that she must make the decision as to which one it would be. She made the choice and lived out the rest of her life bearing a deep sense of guilt. (The story is, of course, similar to William Styron's *Sophie's Choice*, but evidence indicates that such "choices" were offered to many women in the Nazi concentration camps.)

2.   Ada contracted AIDS through sexual intercourse with a bisexual male. She knew she was infected, but she refused to curtail her promis-

cuous behavior because gratifying her strong sexual drives dominated her will. She never told her many partners that she was dying of AIDS.

3.   Dewey spent the better part of the evening at the bar of the country club. By 11:30 he was drunk. His friend Ernie told him to call a taxi, but Dewey insisted he was fine. Ernie, not exactly sober himself, did not pursue the matter. They got in the car and drove off. After weaving all over the road, they turned a corner and hit a wet spot on the pavement that sent the car skidding. Dewey couldn't recover control and smashed into a parked car in which Mary and Joe were sitting. Mary and Joe were killed instantly and Ernie was critically injured. Dewey staggered away from the crash unscathed. He was only ticketed for driving while intoxicated because the victims' car was unlit and irregularly parked. The next evening Dewey was back at the bar stool in the country club complaining to the bartender about the fact that the homeowner on that corner had over-watered his lawn causing the puddle in the street. "And during a drought, too!" (Based on an actual Texas case.)

4.   Lt. Charles took his company into a small village in the Mekong Delta in Vietnam in 1967. The day before, he had lost three members of the company when they had stumbled on a booby trap. The three were his best friends. He had been ordered by Captain Miller to clean out the village and destroy any enemy weapons caches they uncovered. He knew that such orders usually meant that the villagers were to be rounded up and transported elsewhere, but Captain Miller had not specified how the cleanup was to be accomplished. Lt. Charles ordered his troops to gather all the villagers: old men, women, and young children, in a field outside of the village. He then ordered that they be shot, and he participated in the killings. Captain Miller arrived on the scene and joked, "So this is your idea of a clean sweep? Burn the bodies and get out of here." Lt. Charles was later court-martialed for the wanton murder of the villagers. He argues that he was just following orders and that his superior not only was aware of his actions, but approved of them. (Based on the My Lai massacre during the Vietnam War.)

5.   While cruising down 6th Street, John Jones carried a bag of fireworks he had illegally transported into the state. He'd brought them for his children to celebrate the 4th of July. As he ran towards the station to catch the last train to his home, he lost his grip on the package. As it hit the sidewalk, the fireworks inside began exploding. A woman wheeling a baby carriage became so terrified by the explosions, she lost control of the carriage. It rolled out into traffic. A driver trying to avoid hitting it swerved into the path of a truck. In the resulting crash two people were seriously injured. (In the famous case of *Palsgraf v. Long Island Railroad* [New York Court of Appeals, 1928] a similar scenario was used by Judge Andrews to explain his dissenting opinion.)

6.   Karen's father hated her mother. He plotted to kill his wife for months. He settled on putting poison in her tea. He did so as Karen

fetched the cookies and cakes. She returned and, while passing around a plate, she tipped over her mother's teacup. Her father became incensed, lost control, and started throwing things around the room. Alarmed neighbors called the police. When they arrived and examined the room, they discovered the poisoned tea on the table. Karen's mother, when she learned of the failed attempt to poison her, grasped Karen to her. "You saved my life."

7. The oil tanker *Exxon Valdez* hit a reef in Prince William Sound off the coast of Alaska. The captain of the tanker had been drinking and left the ship in the hands of an inexperienced mate. Upon learning of the oil spill, Exxon released a statement disclaiming responsibility, but assuring everyone that it would undertake extensive cleanup operations. They laid all the blame on the captain and the crew, though they arranged for the captain to fly to New York before any charges against him were filed in Alaska.

With these examples in mind, let us try to formulate the way responsibility is ascribed.

## Ascribing Responsibility

To ascribe responsibility is for some person to identify another person as the cause of a harmful or untoward event, because of some action that was performed by that other person, and in light of the fact that the person that was identified occupied a certain type of position or role or station and cannot support an acceptable defense, justification, or excuse for the action.[1]

In the seven examples we have cited, Charles and Miller have specific roles in the military chain of command. Hanna is a mother, and her actions occur within that institutional role. The tanker captain fills yet another institutional role. Dewey's role as driver is not institutional in any normal sense of the term. Still, by getting behind the wheel he does take on the role of a driver, and that carries with it certain requirements, some set by law, others by common sense, etc.

It is important to note that one does not always assume a role voluntarily, but that does not generally weaken the hold that the requirements of the position exert over one's actions in the role. Hanna may not have chosen to become a mother. Soldiers are often drafted. Some philosophers might also argue that there are certain basic roles and, so, certain basic requirements that none of us can escape. One such role is that of a human being (or, at least, a mature, rational human being). Because we are humans, we have certain obligations; or, because we are rational, certain duties fall to us.

Defenses come in two general forms. Either they justify what was done or they excuse it. To justify it is to point out that, under the circumstances, it was the proper or the best thing to do. Hanna might have consoled herself about the loss of one of her twins by noting that she was able to save one, and that under the circumstances that was the best she could do. A similar approach is often taken to justify the dropping of the atomic bombs over Hiroshima and Nagasaki. The argument is that the act, horrendous as it may have been in isolation, nonetheless saved thousands of American lives and shortened the war.

Excuses are rather different from justifications. To excuse your actions, you not only have to admit doing them, but that it was wrong to have done them. Still, an excuse, while admitting the wrongdoing, claims that you didn't do the deed straightforwardly, or boldfacedly, or in full knowledge of what you were doing. Rather, an excuse pleads that other factors intervened, causing your actions, and so you are not directly the instigator. Lt. Charles might claim he was under the duress of superior orders; Dewey might plead that he was drunk or that unavoidable road conditions or the victims' carelessness were at fault; Hanna might say that she had no real choice in the matter; Ada could say that she was driven by impulses over which she had no real control. Excuses may not always get us completely off the hook; indeed they may seldom do so. Most excuses mitigate, but do not exonerate, the responsibility that is ascribed. Suppose that Ada says that she just felt compelled to have sex, despite knowing that in doing so she was probably spreading the fatal disease. We might be persuaded that the sexual urges in her were so strong as to weaken any will she might have had to act in a less risky way, but it is unlikely we would exonerate her completely. To do that, we would have to believe that she couldn't have controlled her urges. (The discussion of excuses is taken up in detail by J. L. Austin in Chapter 2.)

What we mean by the cause of the harmful event can also be troublesome. In tort law we find the doctrine of proximate cause is often used to handle spatial and temporal distancing problems. Think of our fifth case. Remember that it is based on an actual case in American law. The fact that Jones dropped the fireworks, actually, the fact that Jones was running to catch the train, or, maybe, whatever made him late and prompted him to run—perhaps his watch had stopped because the battery died, and he noticed the time on a bank sign—begins a chain of causally linked events that ends in two vehicles crashing and injury to two people. Was Jones's dropping the package the cause of the harm? In one sense it surely seems that it was, but that may be a result of the way the story is told. Somewhere a line must be drawn that limits how far back it is reasonable to pursue a causal chain. In any event, the exploding firecrackers are not the only cause of the crash, and insofar as a number of other links in the chain might have been broken by events or actions that did not occur, it might be thought to be a bit extravagant to hold that

Jones's dropping the package of fireworks was *the* cause of the ensuing harm. On the other hand, in the circumstances, the dropping of the package seems to be an essential part (a *sine qua non*) of the process that culminated in the crash.

Undoubtedly we will want to refine the matter of causation that qualifies one, through one's actions, for responsibility. Will a reasonable person or a reasonable criterion of foreseeability suffice to eliminate remote causal links? Probably not. Or at least there will remain a substantial number of cases in which we will still hold someone responsible for an act that causes an unhappy event, despite the fact that that person or persons could not have foreseen the outcome and a reasonable person would probably not have acted differently. We might wonder if Jones's fault is not so much dropping the firecrackers as having them in the first place. But should responsibility for one act, albeit an illegal one, entail responsibility for all events that follow from it? Is that why, in many cases, drunk drivers are held to account for the harm they cause, though they are incapable at the time of foreseeing the likely outcome?

The causal matter has another side that is evident in the story of Karen and the poison. She most clearly is the causal agent in saving her mother's life, but she did so only because she was clumsy. Still, she satisfies the causal condition. Hence, if asked who is responsible for preventing the father's plot, we should correctly respond that Karen is. To the different question, whether Karen should be held responsible for doing so, meaning, in this case, should she be praised or credited with saving her mother's life, we are likely to say "no." In cases of this sort we turn the exclusion criteria inside out. If the event is bad, we look for reasons why it wasn't done intentionally, or deliberately, or on purpose. If it was good, we look for evidence that it was intentional. It is a rather intriguing feature of our practices, to which we will later return, that lack of intention to bring about the good outcome almost always defeats the ascription of moral praise and credit, but it does not do so in a substantial number of cases when the outcome is bad, harmful, or injurious. In short, negligence has no counterpart on the positive side of the ledger.

Consider the case of the tarnished hero. He is strolling in the park when he spots a young woman being attacked by two hulking brutes. Dashing to her rescue, he pummels the attackers to submission. The story hits the news media with a bang. At last, someone has been found willing to go to the aid of a person in distress, someone willing to risk life and limb for the sake of others. When interviewed, however, our hero reveals that he knew the attackers and they owed him money, and he'd sworn to beat them up when next he saw them. The fact that they were attacking a defenseless woman was of no consequence to him. Lucky for her that he was there, but had he not had a grudge to work off on the attackers, he wouldn't have intervened. He might even have joined them. After all, they used to be his friends!

Once we learn all of that, his actions seem to warrant no praise. Accidental or unintended good samaritanship is hardly the opposite of negligent harm causing. There is probably a very practical reason why that is the case. Identifying the responsible party when harm or injury has been caused is much more important to social life than offering praise to do-gooders. When harm occurs, costs are generally incurred, and the matter of cost-bearing is crucial to the welfare and well-being of individual members, and to society at large.

## Responsibility Practices

There seem to be three practices central to our social system that require the ascription of personal responsibility. If we're going to have a world without responsibility, we need to get rid of such practices, or to alter them radically. One is to determine who merits punishment or reward. The second is to set the targets of burden-shifting, and the third is to identify appropriate subjects of blame and praise. Although these three uses of the ascription of responsibility may often converge on the same person, to ascribe responsibility for the purpose of punishing is a very different moral enterprise from ascribing it for purposes of assessing the costs of harm or injuries suffered. And both of those practices are separable from using it to identify whoever is at fault when things go wrong. Simply put, we could stop using any two of the three practices, and we would still need to ascribe responsibility. Notice how we regularly draw distinctions between the three practices. Take the case of the Exxon oil tanker. Exxon may well be assessed the financial burden of compensating the state of Alaska, as well as those dependent on the wildlife in Prince William Sound for their living, while the captain and his crew may be blamed for the oil spill. Punishment may be meted out to the captain, but not the crew; or it may be meted out only to Exxon.

The difference between punishment and burden shifting (or compensation) is reflected in the distinction between punitive and compensatory damages in tort law, or, more basically, between criminal and tort liability. In *Prosser and Keeton on the Law of Torts*,[2] the distinction between tort and criminal liability is explained in terms of the interests affected and the remedies provided by law. Punishment in criminal law is designed to protect the interests of the public. That protection may be achieved either by eliminating the offender from society (permanently or for a limited period of time), or by reforming the offender, or by deterring others from committing similar crimes. The interests of the victim are not primary and may not even be considered in many criminal proceedings. Society, not the victim, prosecutes; and, if the language of debt is used, it is the "debt to society" that is paid, not restitution to the injured party. In tort law, on the other hand, the action is brought by the injured person to gain compensation for the damage suffered. The law in tort cases serves to enforce the judgment won by the injured party against the harm-causer. Society at large has only a kind of "rooting-interest" in the proceedings. The dominant notions are restitution and compensation. Successful prosecution of a criminal offense against a harm-causer does not guarantee that the injured party will win a compensatory award in tort. But the awards in tort, usually monetary, are primarily to address the damaged interests of a private person, and not the concerns of society at large.

There has developed a secondary level of damages in tort that are not directly related to compensation. That is the area of punitive damages. Such awards are intended to punish or discourage the commission of acts comparable to the injurious one for which the suit was brought, and so constitute an invasion of criminal law into the field of compensation. The award of punitive damages is generally dependent, however, on the injured party's proving that more than the commission of the tort was involved in the injury. "There must be circumstances of aggravation or outrage, such as spite or 'malice,' or a fraudulent or evil motive . . . or such a conscious and deliberate disregard of the interests of others that the conduct may be called willful or wanton."[3] For that to have occurred, the border between individual and social interests must surely have been crossed. In any event, a clear distinction should be made between compensatory and punitive purposes in ascribing responsibility.

The crucial point to be gleaned is that the practice of holding people responsible for things that happen, and hence the concept of responsibility itself, depends for its sense on the purposes or ends to which we put it, the practices in which it is integral and which also depend on it. If there is no longer a reason to punish people; or if there are good reasons to view as unjustified the punishing of people for what they do; or if we cannot justify the sort of burden-shifting that is characteristic of our compensatory system; or if the evaluation of character is unfair or unwarranted or inappropriate, then responsibility ascription will be either meaningless, useless, silly, perverse, or a waste of time. Hence, the ascription of responsibility, no matter how complex it turns out to be internally, ultimately depends for its sense on the adoption of a certain set of practices and institutions. As there is no logical necessity for our having adopted those practices and institutions, the door for creating a world without responsibility is thrown wide open to the skeptic.

## Introducing Doubts about the Responsibility Practices

Those who would do away with responsibility have at least two strategies: (1) they can attack the existing practices by offering morally better alternatives that do not utilize responsibility ascription, or (2) they can show that the very purposes for which the practices exist are dependent upon untenable beliefs. In the latter case, no substitute practices are needed.

Someone taking the second tack might argue that punishment and blame are inappropriate because people cannot help what they do, and we should not hold people responsible for things they could not avoid doing. Most will agree that it is morally wrong to hold people responsible for things that were not in their power to alter. So if all events are strictly determined, people are never really free to act in ways other than they do. To punish or blame or assess people for the costs of harm they could not avoid doing is cruel, unjust. The determinist's (or necessitarian's) argument is difficult to refute on the level of physical events. Causal regularity is central to our explanatory and judicative enterprises. But the determinist needs to show that all human behavior is also determined by prior events in a way that excludes the possibility that a human being could change outcomes by choice. That is not so easy to do, as a large body of literature on the compatability of free will and determinism demonstrates. (Discussions of these issues are the focus of Chapter 3.)

The person who would bring an end to our responsibility practices, however, need not go so far as to destroy the basic belief in human free action. All that needs to be shown is that the practices based on this belief are flawed. One way to do just that would be to defend the view that, at least, criminal behavior is not free. If that is true, then punishment is immoral, given the principle that it is wrong to hold people responsible for what they could not have prevented themselves from doing.

Those who would attribute all criminal activity to social conditions or to psychological factors beyond the criminal's power generally opt for alternatives to punishment. We still, however, will want to separate the criminals from the non-afflicted, normal members of society, so mental wards and asylums would have a role to play in the non-punishment society. Still, even though behavior might need to be very severely restricted, it would not be punishment. Offenders would be treated for their own good or for that of society, but not as retribution for their criminal activity. The disease and not its symptoms would be the target of the therapy and the reason for detention.

There is certainly something appealing in what sounds like a very humane way to handle criminal offenders. But insofar as the techniques of the asylum may be nearly indistinguishable from those of the prison, the real difference between the two approaches comes down to a matter of the description of social intentions. The reason it is not punishment is only because our intent is not to exact an eye for an eye; rather, it is to treat the disease even if during the treatment an eye or two is lost.

Serious doubt may be introduced as to whether we can simply substitute therapeutic practices for punishment without significant moral and social losses. J. L. Mackie once argued that retributive needs are natural to us. It's in our genes, as it were. In any event, according to Mackie, embedded in the concept of wrongness is the belief that "a wrong action calls for a hostile response."[4] This is an important notion. We may capture it in what we may call the rule of retaliation (RR). Clearly RR advocates, even mandates, doing harm to someone. Is this a moral rule? It may be the only one that a moral system can allow. Moral systems generally try to prevent harm-causing; they do not require it.

Is RR optional? Imagine a morality that includes no conception of wrong. To generate the concept of wrongness, however, we may need the concept of deserved retribution. J. L. Mackie maintains that for any moral system, minimally, an act is wrong if it (1) causes harm, (2) is forbidden, and (3) requires a hostile response. All three elements must be present and necessarily connected for full-blooded wrongness. In a boxing match, for example, one fighter may do considerable harm to another, but as long as the match is conducted within the sporting rules, the harm caused is not forbidden and so is not wrong. It is, in fact, often praised.

Mackie believes that we have "an ingrained tendency to see wrong actions as calling for penalties."[5] He believes that there is a biological (or rather a sociobiological) explanation of the origin of our feelings of resentment of moral wrongdoing. I think the case for the rule of retaliation can be persuasively made in a less sentimental way. To do so, let us adopt the familiar thought-experimental device of imagining what human beings would be like in the situation in which there is no civil government and individuals must look out for themselves. Thomas Hobbes, the seventeenth-century political theorist, calls such a situation the state of nature. He describes it as:

> If any two men desire the same thing, which nevertheless they cannot both enjoy, they become enemies; and . . . endeavor to destroy or subdue one another. . . . Hence it comes to pass that . . . if one plants, sows, builds . . . , [an invader] may probably be expected to come prepared . . . to dispossess and deprive him, not only of the fruit of his labor, but also of his life or liberty. And the invader again is in the like danger of another.[6]

Imagine that in such a Hobbesian state of nature one person, Tom, is harmed by an invader, John. John has poked out Tom's eye while trying to steal some food. Tom grabs a stick, chases down John, pokes out one of his eyes, and takes back the food. John would have no doubt that his earlier aggressive actions provoked Tom. The harm caused by Tom in response to the harm he endured probably will discourage John from repeating the raid on Tom. Both will realize that retaliation benefits the retaliator. Hence, if people commit themselves to acting prudentially, they would have overwhelming reasons to independently adopt a retaliatory strategy. The retaliatory strategy is, of course, reactionary. It counsels an eye for an eye, TIT FOR TAT, but it does not provide advice about the first move for either Tom or John. It tells them only what to do if the other invades. It does not directly counsel not invading. Invading, in fact, is the rationally dominant move for either Tom or John to make if (1) he does not expect the other to be able to retaliate *or* (2) he does not know the other has adopted a retaliatory strategy, *or* (3) this is an isolated, unrepeatable situation.

Game theorists have shown that TIT FOR TAT is a relatively successful strategy for players of games of the iterated Prisoner's Dilemma variety.[7] A Prisoner's Dilemma is a two-person game in which each player has to independently make one of two choices. Let us define the choices of Tom and John as either to cooperate with one's neighbor (that is, let him alone to plant, sow, build, etc. and enjoy the fruits of his labors), or to take a hostile action against him: to invade and deprive him of those fruits and his life or liberty. If Tom and John cooperate, the two will create a stable, relatively secure communal environment. It will, however, always be true that if one is cooperative and the other is an invader, then the invader will reap the greatest immediate benefits and the cooperator will suffer greatly. It looks as if it should always be rational to be an invader rather than a cooperator. Of course, if each attacks the other, neither will benefit, both will suffer. The dilemma is that rationality, defined as acting to maximize one's interests, will lead both players to the worst outcome, rather than the best.

Consider the following version of the dilemma:

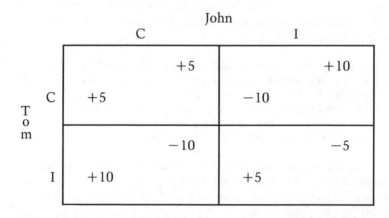

If we assign these arbitrary numbers (or values) to the outcomes for both John and Tom when each plays out his choice, the dilemma is graphically obvious. If one invades when the other is cooperative, the invader realizes the maximal outcome he can achieve. Even if each invades against the other, the loss to each is not as great as it would be if he cooperated while the other invaded. Invading, therefore, offers a better outcome

(+10 or −5) than cooperating (+5 or −10). The worst one can do is −5, but the worst that can happen from cooperating is −10. The gains are also greater from invading than from cooperating. Invading, therefore must be the dominant rational strategy. At least this is true if there is only one play of the game and the players have no knowledge of each other's choices before they simultaneously play them.

Life, however, is not a series of isolated one-play games. We do, of course, find ourselves in a number of such situations when we are rather certain we will never meet the other person again and must decide upon a cooperative or hostile move. Travelers regularly have to make such decisions. Still, much of our experience with others is protracted over time through many plays. The dilemma can be iterated. Does that change the rational strategy? Be an invader, make a big profit; be a cooperator, try to achieve social stability? Tom and John are neighbors and no government affects their behavior. We may assume that they will have many opportunities to make invasion decisions *vis-à-vis* each other. Each decides on a strategy for those interactions; and, as the play will not usually be simultaneous, their strategies must incorporate the need to react to the choices made by the other. What sort of long-term strategy should each adopt?

Let us say that John reasons that the number of plays of the game is unimportant. He has no idea how long Tom will stay in the neighborhood, so each play is as likely as another to be their last engagement. He knows he will always do better if on their final interaction (or play) he invades, and, as that is true of the final play, it will be true of every other play. This is generally referred to as the "rollback" argument. It is clear that on the last play there is no reason for John to try to persuade Tom that he is cooperative. But Tom knows that as well, so the last play isn't really the last play in which choosing to cooperate is a lively option. The second-last play is. But no, the same argument applies, and so the lively option of cooperating rolls back to the third-last play. And so on, until one returns to the first play, where it will also be rational to invade and no cooperation between John and Tom will be achievable by appeal to their rationality.

But John and Tom have no idea when their last interaction will occur, so the rollback cannot be started. Still, it does not seem to be rational for either to cooperate on the first move.

Assume that Tom is about to make the first move. He would prefer a long-term cooperative arrangement with John to a single invasion success, since such an invasion will more than likely be followed by retaliatory invasions by John. Still, he has no way of ensuring that John will not regard any cooperative play by him as an invitation to invade. Invading, after all, is the rational move. Tom is no fool. What strategy should Tom adopt? Following Hobbes' recommendation and his own realization that he is likely to do better over the long haul if both he and John cooperate, Tom decides on two simultaneous actions. He will cooperate and announce a strict retaliatory policy if John does not also cooperate. Simply, he will cooperate on the first move and then on all subsequent moves do whatever John does on his previous move. Tom has, in effect, adopted a TIT FOR TAT strategy.

Robert Axelrod[8] has shown with empirical studies that TIT FOR TAT players cannot do better than those playing other strategies, and they cannot do better than dyed-in-the wool cooperators. But a TIT FOR TAT policy will produce far better results against all other strategies when those non-TIT FOR TAT players also interact with each other.

The reason for that outcome is that TIT FOR TAT is what Axelrod[9] calls a "robust strategy." Unlike the other strategies, TIT FOR TAT is stable across a population of players. What this means is that if all the players in a region have adopted TIT FOR TAT as their approach to interactions with each other, then no other strategy of play chosen by any new player can do better. Non-TIT FOR TAT players cannot remain in the region.

In short, a strategy that seeks cooperation, never initiates invasion, but rapidly responds hostilely to hostility, then immediately returns to cooperation once the other has done so, is the collectively most stable that people can adopt. Such a strategy of human interaction incorporates as a central element the rule of retaliation.

It really doesn't matter whether TIT FOR TAT (and RR that is embedded in it) is adopted through a rational calculative process, or via natural selection. The point is that the adoption by individuals of a retributive strategy will dominate. And as cooperative retaliation by a community of TIT FOR TAT develops, a community of those committed to RR is very likely to form. Such a community may be expected to emphasize notions of cooperation and non-harm in the principles it adopts for intercommunal life. Hence, though founded on a principle of positive harm-causing (RR), a punishment practice, their morality will be dominated by principles antithetical to such positive hostile displays: those deeds they will punish.

This suggests that adoption of punishment practices is a precondition for the stable community to which the other principles of morality are addressed. If that is the case, then responsibility ascription will not be something that can be eliminated. RR requires identifying the responsible party. Responsibility ascription may be foundational to morality as we understand it. This would account for the fact that non-punitive methods of handling offenders are typically viewed as threats to society by the majority of people.

Being deprived of punishment for one's misdeeds also can produce a feeling of utter worthlessness, as if one's life could be dismissed with an expression of forgiveness. Nowhere is this more vividly portrayed than in Eugene O'Neill's *The Iceman Cometh*. Theodore Hickey, a besotted traveling salesman, describes his relationship with his wife:

> No one could convince her I was no good. . . . I'd admit things and ask her forgiveness, she'd make excuses for me and defend me against myself. She'd kiss me and say she knew I didn't mean it. . . . I never could learn to handle temptation. I'd want to reform and mean it. I'd promise her, and I'd promise myself and I'd believe it. I'd tell her, it's the last time. And she'd say, "I know it's the last time, Teddy. You'll never do it again." That's what made it so hard. That's what made me feel such a rotten skunk—her always forgiving me. . . . She'd never complain or bawl me out. . . . Christ, can you imagine what a guilty skunk she made me feel! . . . If she only hadn't been so damned good—if she'd been the same kind of wife I was a husband. . . . It got so every night I'd wind up hiding my face in her lap, bawling and begging forgiveness. And, of course, she'd always comfort me and say, "Never mind, Teddy, I know you won't ever again." . . . I couldn't forgive her for forgiving me. I even caught myself hating her for making me hate myself so much. . . . It got so sometimes when she'd kiss me it was like she did it on purpose to humiliate me, as if she'd spit in my face! . . . So I killed her.[10]

Hickey craves his just desserts. He equates not receiving them with not mattering, not being treated as a full-fledged responsible individual, and that constitutes more than humiliation. It is psychic annihilation. A fitting punishment would have at least made him feel like a person. Just as Dostoyevsky's Raskolnikov[11] desires punishment for his deeds, so too does Hickey require retribution. He sees his murder of his wife as both putting her out of the misery of having to forgive him and as an act of self-defense, though one for which he may be sure to be retributively punished—something he welcomes. Retributive punishment may be selected as a crime-reduction device, as a benefit to the retaliator, but it also satisfies a person's deep-seated needs to be identified with his or her actions in a way that alternative crime control schemes do not. (There is certainly something of the notion of responsibility for character and actions in these needs, as will be discussed in Chapter 7.)

Retributive punishment may have been replaced in the thinking of penologists in this century by rehabilitation theories that are less dependent on responsibility ascription. But ordinary folks still tend to see the appropriateness of penalties as linked to a backward-looking finding of responsibility. The elimination of responsibility ascriptions would be more acceptable if we had no reason to single out particular persons for purposes of punishing their harm-causing. It may, of course, be disputed whether today's penal sanctions are even punishments. Regardless of this, practical considerations may conspire with theory to shake the concept of responsibility from its retributive foundations. With the mounting rate of crime, the social costs of using broad retributive measures may soon exceed (if they do not already do so) any benefits they are supposed to provide. The penal system is bursting with prisoners, and many reformers urge that social benefit considerations must displace matters of deserts. Concern about the likelihood that the convicted felon will be a continuing threat to the community is taking priority over matching the punishment to the crime, over the offender's right to be punished, or the victim's right to retaliate or have society retaliate for invasions that offend against the conditions of social stability. In a world without responsibility there will be no punishment, but such alternatives as rehabilitation, therapy, education, and isolation will be possible so long as the offender is not held responsible for the crime. Perhaps attributions of causal responsibility will still need to be used, but they will bear no moral stigma.

## Blaming Practices

If the practices of punishment that depend upon the ascription of responsibility were to be replaced with a set of less costly institutions that ignore responsibility but maintain social stability, blaming practices might remain. "You won't be punished, but you're to blame for the injury."

Blame has at least three senses, the most basic of which identifies the cause of an unwanted or unhappy event. It functions like the ascription of causal responsibility. In another sense, to blame is just to speak certain kinds of sentences or phrases that express disapprobation, disfavor, irritation, animadversion. The vocabulary of blame is important, but it is the third sense that provides one of the primary purposes of responsibility. To use blaming expressions in this third sense is to hold accountable. To blame is to assert that the actions of a person were one of the causes of an untoward event and that the person in question has no acceptable excuse for those actions, as well as to express a negative evaluation of the event and the disapprobation with which the event *and* the person is viewed. Blaming, in this full-blooded sense, is to hold the person blameworthy. In Hume's words, it is to be concerned with "the quality or character from which the action proceeded." Blaming is a finding of fault in the character of the person blamed. (Chapter 6 focuses on various aspects of blaming.)

Hanna may not be blamed for choosing one child over the other because her choice does not evidence a fault in her character. Dewey, on the other hand, is blameworthy. His drunken harm-causing is evidence of a moral defect in his character.

What would be lost were we to eliminate such character evaluations from our repertoire of practices? Let's abolish this sort of blaming. What would we be doing? Basically, we would stop keeping moral records on each other and we would stop expressing our evaluations of each other's characters. But can we just quit? What would our social lives be like if we never blamed?

We still could punish. When Tom plays the TIT FOR TAT strategy against the invader John, his actions constitute a positive hostile punishment for John's invasion. But he need not blame John for invading. After all, John was acting rationally by invading. To blame him in the full-blooded sense would be to judge acting for reasons of rational self-interest as a character fault. The disciples of the gospel of free enterprise would surely object, and with good reason. Ada, on the other hand, normally would be both punished and blamed for knowingly spreading AIDS. The inability to control one's sexual desires, even among teenagers, is a character fault. But why do we bother to assess her character? People with certain religious beliefs might tell us that this is none of our business. Only God is in a position to evaluate character. All we can do is take people as we find them. But such a world might be very difficult to imagine. On what bases would we establish any kind of long-range relationships with other people? We would have no sense of the moral record, the character, of those with whom we associate. Trust, loyalty, friendship, and most other relational concepts depend on the assessment of characters and the keeping of moral accounts. A society robbed of lasting deep-seated relations hardly could be expected to endure. Every interaction would be independent, ahistorical, momentary. Responsibility ascription as the foundation of blaming gives us the robust social world in which we live.

## Compensation Practices

We might be able to live in a world without blaming or retributive punishment, though our lives would be rather solitary and unstable. That world would still have responsibility ascriptions if it had practices that were used to allocate the costs of compensatable harms based on responsibility assessments. By and large, that is what we do today in tort law. The primary issue of tort law is "to determine when loss shall be shifted from one to another, and when it shall be allowed to remain where it has fallen."[12] Tort law is intended to compensate for losses and injuries sustained by one person as a result of the actions of another. Those adjustments are based on a doctrine of liability that to some extent mirrors the basic responsibility formula, though by admitting the concepts of negligence and strict and vicarious liability it also radically departs from the formula in some types of cases. When it does so, it typically divorces liability from intentionality. Prosser and Keeton write:

> The law looks beyond the actor's own state of mind and the appearances which the actor's own conduct presented or should have presented to the actor. Often it measures acts, and the harm an actor has done, by an objective, disinterested, and social standard.[13]

One's behavior may be reasonable from one's own point of view but still create a serious risk to others or actually cause them injury that one could not have anticipated before the event. Or one may do something in good faith, such as trespass across another's land thinking it is one's own property, and the law may force a compensation payment.

Some losses we suffer at the hands of others are just not compensable, though in many cases the tort law will make an effort at restitution. If you damage my reputation by telling my associates I did something heinous that I did not do, I may succeed in a suit for slander against you. The monetary sum you are required to pay me, however, may not restore my good name in the community. Still, the law made an effort to redress the harm done to me.

What is most intriguing about tort law is that we have it at all. Why should we have a practice that allows the shifting of the burdens of loss within the community? Why do we think that those whose actions harm others should be liable to make restitution quite apart from whatever penalties the criminal law exacts on them? Tort law is premised on the fact that generally losses are transferable, but we certainly do not have to assign them to anyone other than the person on whom they originally fall. There is no logical reason why we could not adopt the practice of never shifting losses. When Dewey critically injured Ernie, Ernie was hospitalized, and the bills mounted to astronomical proportions. Why shouldn't Ernie have to pay those bills himself? Two people were seriously injured when a driver trying to avoid a careening baby carriage smashed into them. Those are the breaks! Why should the costs of their medical treatment be transferred to anyone else?

If we were to adopt a non-compensatory approach to all injuries, responsibility ascription would have no role to play in the process. In order to alleviate financial disasters visited on innocent persons, however, we could spread all injury costs equally across the population. Edmund Pincoffs describes such a scheme as follows: "Each citizen contributes an equal amount to a fund that compensates all losses. . . ."[14]

Those that caused the injuries would pay no more than others. A person who suffers an injury would apply to the fund for compensation. The only issue would be an objective finding that a loss of a certain type had been endured.

Such a "no-fault" scheme for compensation might have socially desirable benefits. For example, the overcrowded tort litigation system, for all intents and purposes, could be scrapped. As Pincoffs points out,[15] that could lessen social tensions. On the downside, there is no deterrent element in the no-fault scheme. Many tort cases involve negligence. There would be little motivation for people to guard against negligent behavior.

Since everyone would contribute an equal amount to the compensation fund, it would be regarded by many as unfair to those on the lower end of the income scale. Arguments undoubtedly would be mounted in favor of replacing equal assessments with something akin to our progressive income tax. Deep pockets would be picked to fill the compensation coffers. In fact, deep-pockets theory is already a significant part of tort settlements. The only difference is that now some contributory responsibility for the injury must be shown. A progressive assessment to maintain the compensation fund would only take ability to pay as the determining factor. Could an argument that does not depend on the concept of responsibility be devised to attack the deep-pockets approach? Are there moral grounds independent of responsibility ascription to adopt a no-fault progressive scheme, rather than an egalitarian distribution of costs? Wouldn't it be argued that ability to pay is a morally insufficient reason to assess someone for the costs of injuries to which they had not even a remote causal connection? How could we justify charging a millionaire in Rhode Island with the compensation costs incurred when a poor person in New Orleans injures someone?

The answers may come in purely practical terms. A person has suffered and must be compensated. Bills must be paid and you can't get blood from a turnip! It could be argued that the maintenance of the compensation fund is just another one of the social welfare costs to which tax dollars must go. Hence, any justification of a non-egalitarian taxation scheme will carry this method of compensation with it. Still, dumping the costs on the rich, for no better reason than their ability to pay, will surely seem unfair because they will then suffer a loss that is neither compensated nor a result of their causing injury.

Placing responsibility ascriptions in a dominant position in the compensatory scheme removes the arbitrariness of the cost-bearing and so will satisfy many of our most cherished intuitions about justice, fairness, and dessert. That should be no surprise, for those intuitions are captured in the responsibility-ascriptions formula. It is the arbitrariness of the administration of penalties and costs in a scapegoating or a purely utilitarian scheme, for example, that seems most to offend ordinary people. Even if all of the other citizens of a town would assuredly prosper if one innocent citizen were arbitrarily chosen for torture, or to pay all of their damages, most of us would think it wrong to inflict such costs on the chosen. However, the practical benefits to the majority could be very persuasive.

## A Society without Responsibility

Imagine, then, a society in which all of the reasons to ascribe responsibility to persons have disappeared because in that society there is no punishment, no blaming, and no individual liability to compensate for harms inflicted. Perhaps all criminal offenses are judged to be the symptoms of disease and the perpetrators, when apprehended, are put into rehabilitation centers. All harms or injuries suffered by members of the society due to the actions of other members are compensated by a general fund to which everyone in society must contribute according to some agreed-upon scheme. And all evaluations of character, all fault-findings with respect to persons, are left to the gods. A pleasant place to live? A utopia? Maybe not. As already suggested, a great deal must also be discarded when responsibility is junked. There would be no praise, no blame, no heroism, no friendships built on character evaluation, no concerns on the part of individuals to prevent negligence. A callous disregard for the welfare of others might grow. In short, unless human nature were to undergo an angelic reformation, a society without responsibility ascriptions and their associated practices would be anything but an idyllic place in which to live.

# NOTES

1. See Edmund L. Pincoffs, "The Practices of Responsibility Ascription," *Proceedings and Addresses of the American Philosophical Association* vol. 61, no. 5, June 1988, pp. 825–39.
2. *Prosser and Keeton on the Law of Torts*, W. Page Keeton, gen. editor (St. Paul, 1984).
3. Ibid., pp. 9–10.
4. J. L. Mackie, *Persons and Values*, Volume II (Oxford, 1985), p. 214.
5. Ibid., p. 215.
6. Thomas Hobbes, *Leviathan* (1651), Part I, Chapter 13.
7. Robert Axelrod, *The Evolution of Cooperation* (New York, 1984), Chapter 2.
8. Axelrod, op. cit., Chapters 2 and 3.
9. Ibid., p. 48.
10. Eugene O'Neill, *The Iceman Cometh* (New York, 1940, 1946), pp. 233–41.
11. Fyodor Dostoyevsky, *Crime and Punishment* (1866).
12. P. Keeton, R. Keeton, L. Sargentich, and H. Steiner, *Tort and Accident Law* (St. Paul, 1983), p. 1.
13. Prosser and Keeton, op. cit., p. 536.
14. Pincoffs, op. cit., p. 832.
15. Ibid., p. 832.